# There's Something in the Water

**Leena Bakshi**

Illustrated by Brian Lamont Burgess

D1736807

STEM
4 REAL

**STEM 4 Real** showcases the real life stories of true STEM pioneers that are currently changing the 21st century using children's literature as our vehicle. We are committed to providing culturally relevant STEM teaching and learning strategies through children's literature. We believe that each and every single child, regardless of gender, race, ethnicity, socioeconomic status, religion or creed should be able to see themselves in the fields of Science, Technology, Engineering, and/or Mathematics. It is through our diversity that we can embark on multiple perspectives in order to progress our STEM fields.

*This book is dedicated to all of my students
that have persevered and succeeded,
especially in math and science!*

*It is also dedicated to all of the
hardworking teachers
inspiring today's youth!*

There's Something in the Water
Copyright © 2019 by Leena Bakshi. All rights reserved.
ISBN # 978-0-9994531-0-0

Published by STEM 4 Real
www.STEM4Real.org

No part of this book may be used or reproduced in any manner whatsoever without written permission except in the case of brief quotation embodied in critical articles and reviews.

Illustrations by Brian Lamont Burgess
Design by Monica Thomas for TLC Book Design, www.TLCBookDesign.com

First Edition
Printed in the United States of America

**NEXT GENERATION SCIENCE STANDARDS***

---

**NGSS Performance Expectations:** This reading supports students in **progressing toward** the NGSS Performance Expectation.

**K-LS1-1:** Use observations to describe patterns of what plants and animals (including humans) needed to survive.
*Clarification Statement: Examples of patterns could include that animals need to take in food but plants do not; the different kinds of food needed by different types of animals; the requirement of plants to have light; and, that all living things need water.*

## IN THIS BOOK ...

| Science and Engineering Practices | Disciplinary Core Ideas | Cross Cutting Concepts |
|---|---|---|
| **Analyzing and Interpreting Data** Use observations (firsthand or from media) to describe patterns in the natural world in order to answer scientific questions. | LS1.C: Organization for Matter and Energy Flow of Organisms All animals need food in order to live and grow. They obtain their food from plants or from other animals. Plants need water and light to live and grow. | Patterns Patterns in the natural and human designed world can be observed and used as evidence. |

| CCSS Mathematics | CCSS English-Language Arts |
|---|---|
| **K.MD.A.2** Directly compare two objects with a measurable attribute in common, to see which object has "more of"/"less of" the attribute, and describe the difference. | **W.K.7** Participate in shared research and writing projects (e.g., explore a number books by a favorite author and express opinions about them.) |

*Next Generation Science Standard is a registered trademark of Achieve. Neither Achieve nor the lead states and partners that developed the Next Generation Science Standards were involved in the production of this product, and do not endorse it.*

Tyrone was a boy who loved nature.
He loved being outside and looking at all the patterns he could find.

He especially loved frogs. He observed that frogs come in all shapes and sizes, like this one sitting on the flower!

Some are **big**,
some are **small**.

Some are **yellow**
and some are **green**.

Some have big **black** spots
and others are **clean**.

One day while making his observations
in his grandmother's swamp,
Tyrone saw something strange.

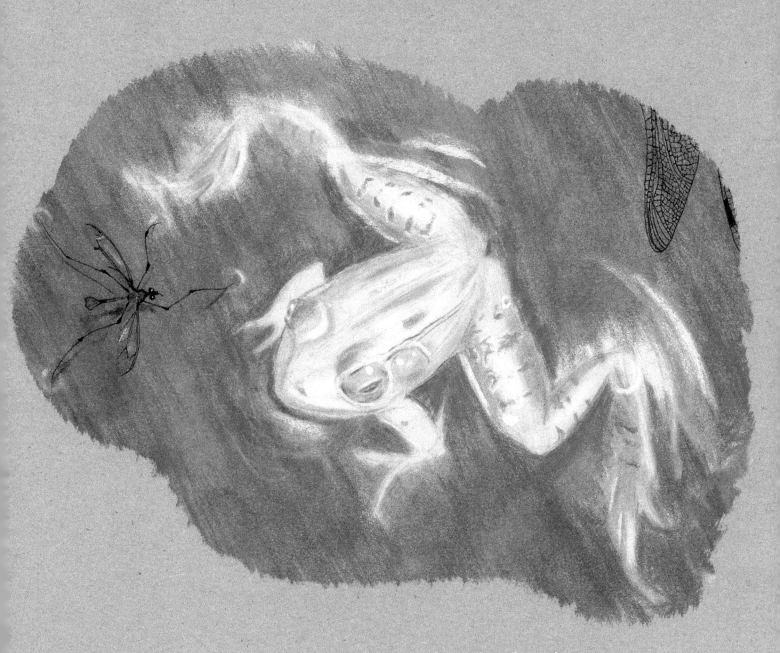

One frog in the swamp looked tired and weak.
His hind legs were twisted and he looked really sick.
He wasn't jumping like the other frogs.

WHY were the frog's legs twisted?
Did he break his legs?
WHY did he look so tired?

Tyrone looked over and saw another frog
with the same twisted legs and tired look.

## "What is happening to all my friends?"

he asked himself.

Tyrone returned from his grandma's house and couldn't stop
thinking about those poor frogs. He went over to the swamp
at his house and saw an entire population of healthy frogs,
jumping and playing in the water.

The frogs are fine here. There are more frogs here too!
Why do the frogs at Grandma's house look so unhealthy?

Tyrone had to find out.
He started a science notebook
and wrote down all of his observations.

He noticed that the frogs next to his grandma's swamp
were very skinny and looked weak.

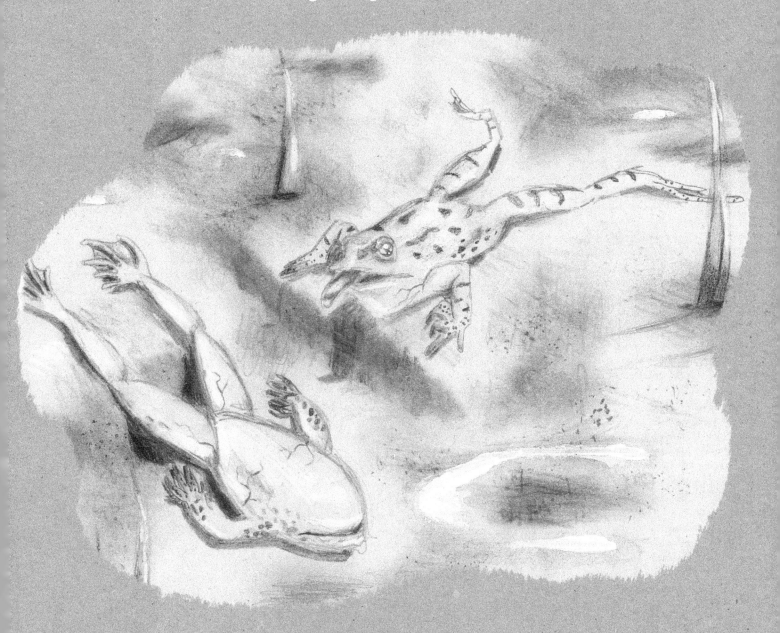

He compared the size of the frogs between his house and his grandma's house.
The frogs at his grandma's house were very tiny!

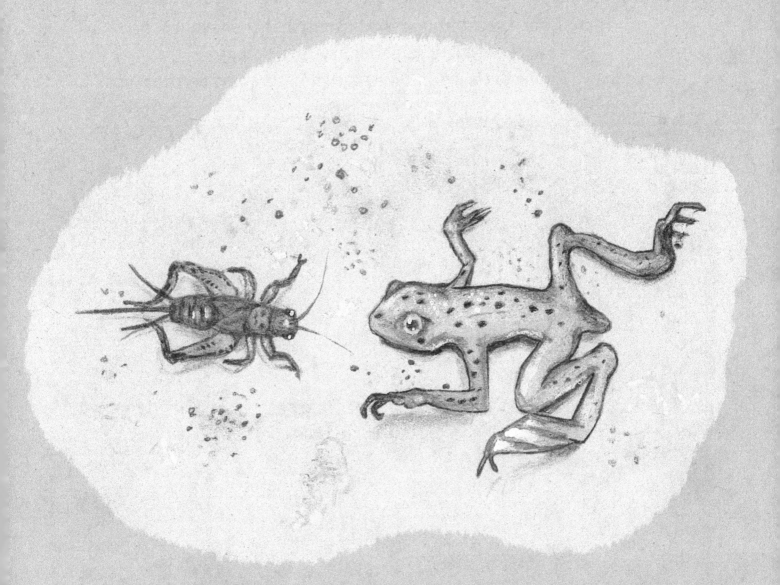

# Look at this frog!

He can't even eat the cricket because the cricket is too big
to eat! Tyrone learned that all animals need food in order
to live and grow. If the frog is not eating, it's not growing!

Then, Tyrone saw through the bushes that the neighbors
were spraying something on their crops.
"Grandma!" Tyrone exclaimed, "What are they spraying on the crops?"

His Grandma answered,
"Baby, they are farmers and they are spraying weed killers
so that the crops can grow big!"

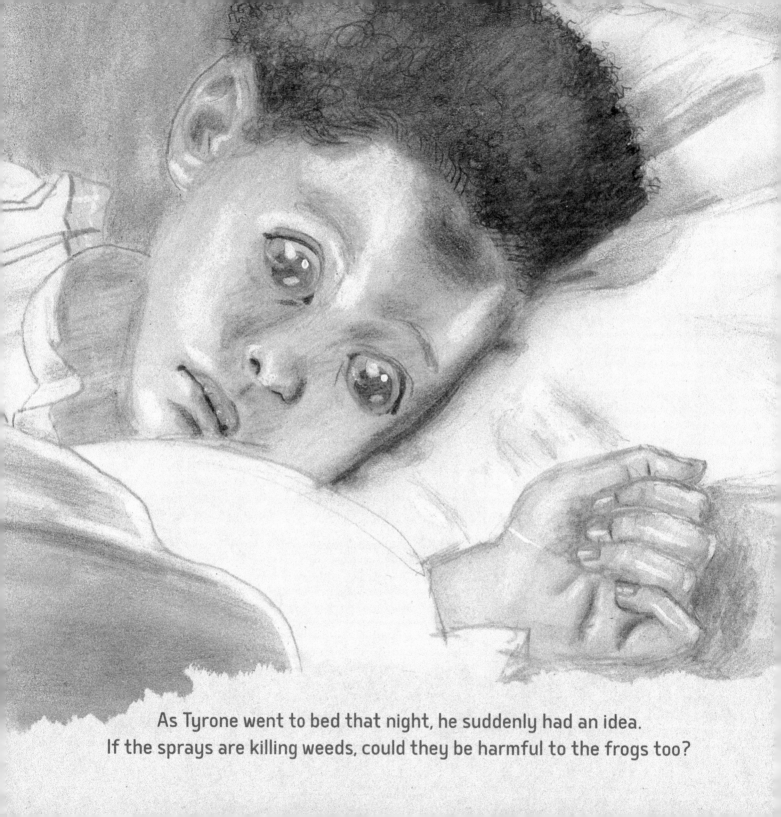

As Tyrone went to bed that night, he suddenly had an idea.
If the sprays are killing weeds, could they be harmful to the frogs too?

Tyrone learned that frogs need food and water to survive.
If the water supply is contaminated, the frogs are going to get sick!

Tyrone asked his grandma to help him collect water samples.
He compared the swamp water from his house to the
swamp water at his grandma's house.

The test showed that his swamp water was normal,
but Grandma's swamp water was not.

Tyrone collected all of his data and compared the patterns of healthy frogs and unhealthy frogs.

Next, Tyrone compared the healthy water and unhealthy water.
He put all his data together in a report and showed it to
his teacher for the annual science fair.

At the annual science fair, Tyrone was nervous to speak in front of everyone, but he knew he had to say something for his frogs. He presented his claim and used his observations as evidence to support his claim.

Tyrone said, "Look at this frog. It has a healthy body,
Now look at this one from this swamp next to the farm,
his head is crooked and his legs are weak!"

All of the judges were impressed with
Tyrone's project and how it related
to his community.

# He was voted first place!

# PH DATA ANALYSIS OF OUR WETLANDS

## RESULTS

CONCLUSION

**FLORA**
EFFECTS:

**DRINKING WATER**
EFFECTS:

**WILD LIFE**
EFFECTS:

CONGAREE SWAMP VS. BERRY SWAMP

Tyrone knew he wanted to pursue science as a career.
He did well in school and applied to Harvard University
writing about his passion for animals.

# Tyrone Hayes, STEM4Real Star

**A**s a child, I never would have imagined that my interest in frogs and my love of animals and plants could lead me to college. Whatever your passion, stick by it! Education…grade school, college, and beyond will give you the power to have choices. Having those choices will allow you to have a job that makes you happy.

Dr. Tyrone Hayes is an American biologist and professor of Integrative Biology at University of California, Berkeley. He is an advocate for the regulation of pesticides and other chemicals that may cause adverse health effects. He has presented hundreds of papers, talks, and seminars on his conclusions that environmental chemical contaminants have played a role in global amphibian declines and in the health disparities that occur in minority and low income populations.

Printed in the USA
CPSIA information can be obtained
at www.ICGtesting.com
JSHW061621151023
50145JS00007B/28